The Christmas Birthday Visit

To Marilyn,

Mary Kathy Hicks

2021

The Christmas Birthday Visit

MARY "KATHY" HICKS

Trilogy Christian Publishers

A Wholly Owned Subsidiary of Trinity Broadcasting Network

2442 Michelle Drive

Tustin, CA 92780

For information, address Trilogy Christian Publishing

Rights Department, 2442 Michelle Drive, Tustin, Ca 92780.

10 9 8 7 6 5 4 3 2 1

Library of Congress Cataloging-in-Publication Data is available.

ISBN 978-1-63769-534-0

ISBN 978-1-63769-535-7 (ebook)

To

My Abba, the God Almighty

My Savior, the Lord Jesus Christ

My Guide, the Holy Spirit

In Loving Memory of

My Sister, Betty Read – at home with the Lord in 2020

INTRODUCTION

As you will read later, this is the one book that I did not want to write. I have enjoyed writing all my life and have many writings both composed and swimming in my head. This book would be the last that I would want to write, more less publish. However, the Lord made it very clear to me that I was to write it. I did so in obedience. I struggled even more when the Lord moved me to submit it to a publisher. I submitted it thinking that maybe I was just to write it but that surely no one would want to publish it. Shocked, I found that it looked like I was to do just that. I struggled, looking for verification from the Lord. Suddenly, some obstacles came in my way. One obstacle required that I learn a new form of submitting to the will of the Lord in an area of my life. Other obstacles required that I step in faith and trust. For these last ones, the Lord provided me answers—my signs. As I sought signs, I remembered from scriptures others who felt inadequate and uncertain, ones such as Gideon. I identified with his needing confirmations. My signs were the days of the numbered yellow flowers and of the eleven hundred dollars. Perhaps, I will feel comfortable sharing about these events in more detail at some future time. For now, I just want the reader to know that this sharing is the result of struggles, submission, signs, faith, searching scriptures, and trust that was slow on my part but loving and steadfast on the Lord's part. I am no one special in my eyes. I have wondered if the Lord is wanting me to share because of all my failures, uncertainties, doubts, and retreats. I remembered how when I read books written by great Christian leaders about how the Lord worked in their lives, that I have wondered about how their stories apply to me, just an ordinary person. I wondered if I am writing for others like me. Perhaps, He wants us to know that we are all special and dearly loved in His sight.

I often have to struggle with what I considered major sins that would bring me under a feeling of condemnation. I would have to cling to "There is therefore now no condemnation to those who are in Christ Jesus, who do not walk according to the flesh, but according to the Spirit. For the law of the Spirit of life in Christ Jesus has made me free from the law of sin and death." (Romans 8:1-2, NKJV) The Lord has always patiently helped me to remember that His sacrifice has taken care of all of these. Perhaps, in writing this He again was showing me His love to draw, encourage, and pull me into His will and plans. I definitely am learning to understand the scripture "My grace is sufficient for you, for My strength is made perfect in weakness." (2 Corinthians 12:9, NKJV)

The Christmas Birthday Visit

I have always loved the Christmas season. As a little girl, I found everything magical, exciting, and spiritual. These three themes filled not only my local neighborhood but also the towns and cities. I sometimes wonder today if the popularity of the "Hallmark" concept of the season tries to revisit these themes even if it does not quite capture them. Although neighborhoods had some visuals of celebration during my childhood, the spirit of the people and the local places of worship seemed to overflow with an inner essence of joy and goodwill. Major displays were primarily in town or city centers. The downtown area had streets lighted and decorated, not like today with all the electronics, but with a tasteful simplicity projecting more of the true spirit of the season while still being like a wonderland to me then. The department stores had large windows with Christmas scenes and animatronics. One store had a succession of windows depicting the Christmas story from the Annunciation to the Escape into Egypt.

The lighting of the large Christmas tree was a wondrous event as well. Families would gather around anticipating the magical moment when the lights showed the splendor of the majestic tree in a city park. Caroling groups took their turns at this event and in subsequent evenings so that families might go again after shopping to hear other caroling groups. I was excited several times to be in groups that sang. Two stores, one local and another in the neighboring town, had a Toyland, each one with its own magic. One had a monorail to ride and another a toy electric train high above that ran the entire circuit of that section.

Until this day, I secretly harbor a wish for such a train and do have a small, less than impressive Christmas train. I have never really been able to recapture the impressive image of these ones from my childhood because towns became large cities which focused more on modern commercialism. I was encouraged one Christmas, as an adult, that a smaller town tried to capitalize on its old style, downtown area with its quaint shops. It still had a Christmas parade with locals making the floats. The shops had friendly owners with hot drinks and treats that were free. One special Christmas while walking and shopping with relatives in that town, we experienced a light snowfall with the sounds of Christmas music and smells of the hot treats emanating from the shops. All did seem full of love, joy, and peace, and all was right with the world.

These marvelous memories centered on faith, family, and fun. The Christmas season was always about Christ's birth. The theme was definitely "For there is born to you this day in the city of David a Savior, who is Christ the Lord" (Luke 2:11, NKJV). Then, it seemed that everyone knew the story of Christ's birth and those who were part of His birth. I know that I felt privileged to have the first name Mary. I especially liked this name at Christmas time. I thought about how wonderful it must have been to be so chosen by God. I thought about how "Then the angel said to her, "Do not be afraid, Mary, for you have found favor with God" (Luke 1:30, NKJV). Thinking back, I was silly about this idea for several reasons. First, most people did not call me that name; family and friends called me by my nickname Kathy. I am actually Mary Katherine. I have always loved my name. I found in school that teachers would call me by whatever had fewer occurrences in the class. One year I might be Mary, another year Katherine, and one year even Mary Katherine. I felt very special that year. Kathy eventually prevailed. Either the teachers liked that name, or they simply gave up trying to have unique names for students. Settling on Kathy was probably for the best because of a second reason. I cannot fit the standard of the Mary of the Bible. I lack such great humility, purity, and faith. Now, I consider how I cannot compare to but do marvel at her faith. When I was young, I was a little closer to that faith, having a beautiful childlike faith. I felt so pleased that I was chosen to play the part of Mary in the Christmas cantata at my elementary school and would later be Mary in the live nativity scenes at church. My first live birth (my first child was stillborn) was almost on Christmas. Although the process began on Christmas, my daughter was born four days later. I remember thinking how special it would be for a child to share Christ's birthday. Since those thoughts, I have discovered that those people born around Christmas actually can feel somewhat overlooked and even cheated by such a birthday proximity. Having children has left me with one point that I can come near to feelings similar to Mary in the Biblical account. These feelings are when I read "And all those who heard it marveled at those things which were told them by the shepherds. But Mary kept all these things and pondered them in her heart" (Luke 2:18-19, NKJV). I have many times, especially in respect to my children, grandchildren, and great grandchildren, "hidden things in my heart and pondered them." As an adult, I have to use the name Mary legally, which has led me to another type of pondering or carefully thinking about things as I make decisions. "Ponder the path of your feet, and let all your ways be established" (Proverbs 4:26, NKJV). Now as I ponder things past, present, and future, I know that I miss the mark of Mary's faith and obedience as she responded to the angel Gabriel as she said, "Behold the maidservant of the Lord! Let it be to me according to your word" (Luke 1:38, NKJV). I am trying to learn from another Mary in the Bible to sit at the feet of Jesus, drawing nearer to Him.

I am more of a Mary than a Martha. I do love to listen and learn. I often feel guilty because I am not always the best hostess. I look for shortcuts to preparing and displaying meals so that I can spend more time interacting with company. I would rather discover and hear new teaching than work behind the scenes. Actually, I will stop or slow the pace of work, straining to understand what is being said if I try to do work while teaching is imparted. Although I believe I need to be more of a Martha, I know that of the two, I would have been and am a Mary. I have felt comforted reading that Jesus said, "Martha, Martha, you are worried and troubled about many things. But one thing is needed, and Mary has chosen that good part, which will not be taken away from her" (Luke 10:41b-42, NKJV). The small part of me that is Martha, the worried and troubled area, does fade away when I listen to the Lord and hear His Word.

As I ponder so many things from Him, my prayer is that He will strengthen my faith and lead my feet. This Christmas writing perhaps shows what lead me to its true meaning. Yes, Christ was very much in Christmas in those days—in public, in the community, in school, and church, especially in the songs.

Singing groups were not limited to only public and organizational gatherings. Caroling could be heard in the neighborhoods with people opening their doors and serving cookies and hot chocolate to the carolers. Most of the songs were religious ones with just a few other classics. I tried keeping this spirit alive as long as possible when I taught in public schools. My French and Latin classes were the perfect venue. I found that students learned vocabulary, grammar, and pronunciation more readily through songs. Students and faculty looked forward to our annual Christmas caroling through the halls. However, as final exams began to come before Christmas break and sensitivity to religious songs increased, the caroling had to end. This was such a sad end. I believe the students missed this celebration as much as I did. I hope that they maintained some of the treasured memories as I have. I have been heartened to see in the last few years some attempts to revive more public caroling that includes the religious songs.

Of course, many might say that media has replaced these singing troupes. Television, social media, and radio provide platforms. Some provide those classic songs. I do search for those I heard so often as a child. I remember that my dad loved "Silver Bells," often singing it to me. "Silent Night," "Oh, Holy Night," "The First Noel," and "Oh, Little Town of Bethlehem" were among my favorites. I marveled at the beautiful sounds of "Ava Marie." Such songs would bring thoughts of how glorious that night must have been at Christ's birth. "And suddenly there was with the angel a multitude of the heavenly host praising God and saying:

'Glory to God in the highest, And on earth peace, goodwill toward men!'" (Luke 2:13-14, NKJV)

Good Tidings! Love came down to be the lamb that would take our place to offer us salvation and amazing grace!

The spiritual theme permeated not only the sounds of Christmas but also the sights of the season. The professionally lighted specials with their choreographed arrangements are beautiful, but there was something uniquely special and in the spirit of the season when neighbors and groups would ban together, very unprofessionally, to sing these favorites. They felt safe to go into neighborhoods and businesses and, amazingly, felt warmly welcomed.

This warmth for the season seemed more personalized, public, and prevalent than today. Houses donned lights, stars, and many even had nativity scenes of their own inside and outside. Some of the outside ones were definitely homemade. I treasured the small nativity scene that my family had. I would arrange it on the mantle and even play with it. I still have a few of those original pieces today though some have chips and many are missing. I lost the baby Jesus for a few years but found Him miraculously one Christmas. I would consider what each must have felt that night. The shepherds heard the news from the angels and went to see. "And they came with haste and found Mary and Joseph, and the Babe lying in a manger" (Luke 2: 16, NKJV). What did Mary hide and consider in her heart? Now, I have several nativities, or crèches, and I am even looking at one right now that remains on a table, having escaped being packing away from last Christmas. I have a small one made in the Holy Land. Although I have never been able to visit there myself, I was given this one after a visit to a Dead Sea Scrolls exhibit. I don't have a large collection but continue to work on it.

I have one that I enjoyed sharing with my grandchildren and soon great grandchildren, "What God wants for Christmas." It is interactive with figures in little boxes that are numbered indicating the order to open them. Each one has a figure to fit into the nativity scene fold out that is included. A booklet has readings to go with each figure. The last box contains a mirror that shows what God wants is you.

What God Wants for Christmas © 2011 by FamilyLife. Used by permission.

Another one I cherish is an inexpensive one that I did with a grandchild. It has figures that the child places on the flat scene surface. Somehow, one of the wise men was lost. A deep cleaning under a sofa revealed the lost character.

I love what these represent: God loves us enough to send His own son to us with the purpose of letting us see that love and with the purpose to sacrifice Himself so that we can be part of His family for now and forever. With such a great purpose behind a nativity scene's symbol, I am not sure if one can ever have enough nativity scenes.

Live nativity scenes were and still are my favorite. As a youth, I loved the live nativity that our church sponsored. All ages contributed to having this scene for the public from just after Thanksgiving to Christmas Eve. We had a stable, hay, live animals, live characters in costumes, except for the baby Jesus (one Christmas a couple did share their young baby a few times on balmy nights), and music. On cold nights, we had to change casts frequently, allowing for food, hot drinks, and body warming between our shifts. We developed strong bonding during these times, especially generationally. We had some of the older members who contributed everything from leading us in building and setting up the stable, providing the animals, playing parts, preparing costumes and snacks to being there for support, protection, and assistance. I loved seeing the families come by to see the live nativity. The children were very excited. Truly, the real meaning of Christmas was a community happening. Of course, other public events included Christmas pageants and musical concerts that, again, were focused on the spiritual side of Christmas. Today, some still exist in religious circles. However, many of the public events are more secular in nature.

It seemed easier in those days to stay focused on the true spirit of the season. We shared food and gifts, especially with those in need. I know my father once was in charge of getting toys from a toy drive out to children. That year, there were many toy animals. I cleaned each one and helped him deliver these. I felt that it was a very special sharing. Sunday school classes often adopted a family to provide for them. Even school classes would often participate in providing for a family. Many such charitable activities do still exist today. However, often the giving can be at a distance from the family. For example, as a class, we would go to that family to present the gifts. Now, we often donate items or money, and an organization or selected individuals deliver these. Those delivering still see the joy when the items are presented, but many of us don't get to see that moment. I do feel the blessing from giving. I realize that large, organized drives probably provide more to a greater number. I just felt the smaller groups giving to the individual added a personalized sense of bonding between all involved. This Christmas, I asked my grandchildren to pick specific items that I would donate to in their honor through Samaritan's Purse. I hoped that doing so would help them feel the joy of personalized giving. I am glad that children are encouraged to participate in any such activity so that they can experience the joy and understanding about giving as a blessing that far outweighs receiving.

Another activity that I particularly liked to do with my father was going to pick out our tree. Live trees have always been special to me. Actually, I often thank the Lord for trees I have right now. I am very concerned that any pruning be by those who value trees and are knowledgeable about this work. One difficult and lonely time for me, I noticed the trees behind my fence blowing almost as though they were clapping. I discovered a wonderful verse that brought me comfort and joy that I treasure even today. "For you shall go out with joy, And be led out with peace; The mountains and the hills Shall break forth into singing before you, And all the trees of the field shall clap *their* hands" (Isaiah 55:12, NKJV). We had many live Christmas trees because it was many years before artificial trees were available, so I had the fun of picking out just the right live tree for much of my childhood. Even the tree lots seemed alive with Christmas atmosphere. We could not put the trees up too early because they would dry out and become dangerous, so timing was critical. We had to be sure we did not wait so late that the good trees were gone. I know we had to be certain that there was plenty of the water for the tree because a dry tree increased the likelihood of a fire. We, also, had to check that lights were turned off and any decorative candles were never left on at night. These rules were as stringent as turning our two gas heaters off at night no matter how cold it might be so that we would not be in danger as we slept. Mother would stay up late to turn them off and rise early to turn them back on in the morning. I would usually stay right in front of one heater in the morning trying to stay warm. I would sometimes dry my hair in front of it and often studied late nights there as well. One time, I fell asleep studying and awoke to the smell of the top of my hair as it singed. Now, back to Christmas trees, the artificial trees appeared to be safer, so we finally switched to those. The artificial silver trees were never the same as the live tree. Today, the newer ones are safer and do have more the look of live trees. As an adult, I wanted to have my children experience live trees. However, I found the artificial necessary when one Christmas my oldest son seemed to have an allergy to live trees. I must say that the life-like look of the artificial trees, safer lights, and automatic timers today are an improvement. I have a device that allows me to talk to my tree, Mr. Christmas. He is voice activated and will turn on and off the lights and even play a number of Christmas songs upon request. The music includes flashing of the lights in time to the music. I guess a few times Mr. Christmas has felt neglected. Hearing some sound that might be close to the oral commands, he activates, becoming frustrated if I do not ask for a song. He then makes a selection and begins playing. I have had a few telephone calls and online meetings interrupted by these impromptu concerts. The only options are to turn him off, wait until a song finishes and give a command, or just enjoy the song. Yes, I believe I might prefer the new technologies and trees but miss the experience of tree selecting. Perhaps, having live-planted trees that can now be safely lighted and decorated combines much of the joy of the past and the present.

Now getting back to my youth, decorating the tree was a major event as we inspected each ornament and placed either a star or angel on top. At first, most ornaments were fragile. A few times, I was devastated when I broke one. I remember the first time we had some spray snow for the tree. I imagined that we had the most wonderful tree ever. I was in charge of ornaments and ice cycles on the lower part of the tree. I helped with the mantle decorations. We did not have special stockings, so I would get one of my dad or brother's socks because they were bigger in hopes of more goodies Christmas morning. Christmas morning fruits, nuts, and maybe a few pieces of candy were the surprises in our stockings. The fruit often included oranges.

Years later, I would learn that the practice of putting oranges in stockings could be traced to a story about St. Nicholas and his throwing bags of gold through a window to save young girls from being sold into what would be slavery because they had no dowry. As a young boy, Nicholas lost both of his wealthy parents. His parents had taught him to follow Jesus. He did so by giving away his money, helping the poor, and performing acts of kindness, especially to children. He became Bishop of Myra. However, he later would be persecuted for his faith and imprisoned. He died on December 6 (the earlier Julian calendar would list December 19). I can see why St. Nicholas Day became associated with Christmas and gift giving. I wonder now if my parents knew about the association with him and put oranges into the stockings because of it. Many items associated with our celebration of the season remain but their spiritual significance is lost. Our candy cane legends trace back to 1670 in Germany and find our crooked-shaped, striped ones in Indiana. These latest ones are symbols for Jesus. One direction shows the staff for the Good Shepherd and the other way is a J for Jesus. The white symbolizes His purity with the red indicating His blood shed for our sins. I have made little ornaments this year with the candy cane and the poem that describes its meaning. Understanding the meaning behind many of our customs could help us focus more on the true meaning of the season. I wish I had learned and shared more in the past and definitely plan to do so more in the future from stockings, candy canes, and all sorts of traditions.

I have definitely expanded my celebration with stockings. Now, I have the traditional red ones with white tops going all the way down the staircase because of the grandchildren, great grandchildren, and ever expanding family. I like to have a stocking for any guest that will be at my house for Christmas. I have some standard gifts in the stockings-candy, small hand lotion and chap stick, and then the unusual or handmade item. One year when some of the older boys were teenagers, I had designer toy cars such as Lamborghinis. I jokingly told them that I bought them all sports cars. I search all year for something unique. One rule is that guests must leave the stockings. This year was one when I was unable to have anyone here. The stocking tradition had to continue. I found inexpensive, though smaller, stockings that could be jammed with items and delivered to people. I may be wrong, but I think that their still having the stocking fun helped not having the physical presence. Sometimes the small, simple things are the most important and the sweetest.

Speaking of sweetness, sweets during my early childhood were generally only for special occasions such as Thanksgiving and Christmas. Oh, we did have homemade ice cream sometimes in the summer and pudding or Jell-O with fruit after meals. Later, the Manor bread man provided sweet options that were probably not very healthy. Christmas was the time for making pies, cakes, cookies, divinity, and brownies. I would try to arrange these treats on dishes to make them look elegant as my child's mind saw them. Another special treat was setting the table with mother's good china, silverware, and crystal. Daddy would often gather nuts, especially pecans. Pecan pies were one of my favorites. We had a few special serving dishes that were used only at this time. I still have some of these dishes. One is a lazy Susan. It has a mended cracked section; however, it has a special place of honor, generating memories of happy times. I must admit that it wasn't only the taste of the food I loved—it was the atmosphere and joy. I imagined that even in our small dining room that our settings were as elegant as anyone else had. Besides the sweets, we had special foods that mother fixed primarily at this time. I loved the feast. As an adult, I tried to recapture some of what I saw as Christmas elegance. I have a few special Christmas items—green trimmed china, green crystal, decorative salt and pepper shakers, and a few odd serving items. None of these were expensive but they seemed as Christmas memory treasures to me. As the family grew and crystal and china was broken, the desire for elegance began to be replaced for the smiles and voices of children, grandchildren, and guests. I still want to have some of the elegance so that the children have memories like mine. However, I have discovered some disposable plates and cutlery that look like china and silver. The red solo cups just do not even provide any semblance to crystal. I would not have enough crystal now anyway. I have found that even the sweets have lost much of their appeal as children have grown into teens, young adults, and adults who are concerned about sugar intake for themselves and their children are restricted to only a few such treats. My chocolate cake with its appearance of snow and Christmas scene atop usually glistens under the crystal cake globe more now as a decoration and less of a treat to be devoured. Thankfully, I am growing, learning that it is less about recapturing loved memories, not that these are wrong, but it is about the love. I am reminded of the scripture, "that their hearts may be encouraged, being knit together in love, and attaining to all riches of the full assurance of understanding, to the knowledge of the mystery of God, both of the Father and of Christ, in whom are hidden all the treasures of wisdom and knowledge" (Colossians 2:2-3, NKJV). My heart and understanding are growing. Although many of the externals might seem the same or even slightly different, I am becoming more attuned to the hidden treasures of the love for my precious ones and to what I so want to share is encouragement and knowledge of what the Father and Christ Jesus offer them. My prayer is for this knitting together in love now and forever. We all need constant reminders that this season is truly about God's gift to the world.

As with most children, my anticipation of gifts on Christmas morning filled the days leading up until then with much excitement. Often, we would be able to open one present Christmas Eve. Mother usually guided which present. Strangely, the present we were allowed to open was often warm pajamas or a robe; warm socks or house shoes sometimes were selected. My favorite pajama was a velveteen set with an oriental style top. I felt luxurious in what I saw as designer lounging attire. The next day, I would open black velveteen slippers with rhinestones on them. I thought that I was the luckiest girl ever. Santa's gifts Christmas morning were limited usually to only one item. However, we might receive additional treasures (such as I just described) from a family member. I remember a few dolls, a stuffed poodle, and toy vacuum cleaner. I would often make presents for family members. Sometimes, I could buy them with money from selling bottles and coat hangers. We had a small center at the corner intersection with a dry cleaner, five and dime store, and small grocery store. I could earn one to two cents in exchange for each bottle or hanger. As early as ten years old, I was babysitting, so I was able to add to these funds for purchases at the corner. The five and dime was a wondrous place because they would let me put things in lay away. The owners were so nice, even letting me occasionally look at what they were holding for me prior to my completing the payment. I did try not to abuse their kindness. The concept of layaway was good for the consumer because the person actually had to finish paying for something before they received the item. In this way, we learned long-term planning and goal gratification. Credit cards became the substitute that lead to possible bad habits as opposed to good ones. I can see the advantages for the businesses but not for the consumers. I guess the alternatives are saving money throughout the year or buying gifts throughout the year. I have tried combinations of both. The downside to buying gifts early is that I must hide them. Then, I must frantically search for them. Some years I fail to find some and have to buy new ones. A few times, years pass before I find the missing presents. I am a little ashamed to admit that finding these a year or two years later is somewhat like uncovering hidden treasure. Despite all my new strategies, I believe it was easier in those earlier times to focus on the spiritual meaning of Christmas even in the gift giving.

These childhood memories were regularly joyous. I can remember only three that were saddened. One was when my parakeet, Bobby, died. The second one was when I had the gift that I had made for my grandmother and was unable to give it to her because she had passed. The third one was one that I didn't really understand the full extent of the sadness until I was older: it was when my brother was overseas as a missionary and did not come home for Christmas. I saw a difference in my mother. She was trying hard to have full joy; however, there was a lacking, a sense of emptiness in her because her son was not there. I fully came to understand her feeling as I, too, years later would experience Christmas without one of my family. I would feel deep loss several times. I would have Christmas without my father and, then, without my mother. I felt the pain of a Christmas after a stillbirth. This Christmas my oldest sister had passed earlier in the year. However, she had assured me that she was ready. I know that she was celebrating with the Lord. Then, painful times marred the holidays because of family issues. One is so painful that I am unable even to write about it. Another one brings back images and feelings of a cold, snowy-icy Christmas that I spent all alone, eating cheesecake and crying. I must say that the Lord really helped me through these most difficult ones. I found a special comfort and nearness with the Lord, perhaps more in the sad times than the joyous ones. "Blessed be the God and Father of our Lord Jesus Christ, the Father of mercies and God of all comfort" (2 Corinthians 1:3, NKJV).

Of course, there were many wonderful ones with family and friends. My favorite times have been watching children excitedly open presents and exclaiming joy at decorations and lights. I have always loved Christmas lights. I have had many special occasions seeing these, even recently going to a Christmas cave. I believe that this must be the most unusual experience. I have gone through unbelievable mazes and decorative drive through settings. I had the opportunity to see lights via a horse drawn carriage. I must admit this ride came close to those imaginings of sleigh bells in the snow from my childhood dreams. Visiting an arboretum with large globes and animatronics of the twelve days of Christmas brought back memories of those store windows of my childhood. I so have enjoyed the special sights, sounds, and the decorating and the gift buying.

I do still like making gifts but just cannot seem to do what I used to do. I remember staying up all night Christmas Eve completing child-sized Raggedy Ann and Andy dolls for two of my children (the third one was not here yet; I often wished that I could have a made a third doll). I stayed up another night to finish a princess dress. My most joyous shopping experience was one year when I had to wait until I received my Christmas bonus before being able to buy any presents. I had a babysitter keep the children so that I could buy all presents the day before Christmas. I had no time to worry about what I was buying. I just bought what I could find and afford. In many ways, it was liberating. My most blessed shopping was when I did not buy anything. It was a difficult Christmas. I did not know how I would be able to do anything. The doorbell rang. Two people were dressed as Mr. and Mrs. Claus. They had gifts and food. To this day, I do not know who they were but thank the Lord for them. I pray I can be blessings as they were. I know helping Angel Trees affords me some opportunity to try to repay that blessed outpouring of love. Love can arrive in many ways.

Christmas cards can help share a message of love during the season. I had a few Christmas times when I printed and used stamps to make Christmas cards. Then, I did a few animated email cards. Lately, I have painted a watercolor and written a poem to print cards. I wondered if I would be able to do a card this year, but I did complete one that can be seen at the close of this writing. One was shared earlier, and I share a couple more here.

Rejoice this Christmas time!
Rejoice all you lambs,
lost, lonely, feeling unloved.
The Saviour is born!
Praise the Lamb who
sacrificed, saving, giving grace!

"Behold! The Lamb of God who takes away the sin of the world!" John
1:29 nkjv
"All we like sheep have gone astray; We have turned, every one, to his
own way; And the Lord has laid on Him the iniquity of us all."
Isaiah 53:6 nkjv

Into a cold, dark world God sent His son, showing the warmth and hope of His love so that this child became a shining light of grace bringing salvation to a lost world!

If we accept this gift of salvation that He offers, we can reflect such love, providing light to the dark and warming the cold!

Again, a new commandment I write to you, which thing is true in Him and in you, because the darkness is passing away, and the true light is already shining.
1 John 2:8

The card on the previous page that presents the snowy mountain scene with small lights inside the isolated houses and the candle reflects several thoughts about the Christmas season that have germinated inside me over time. As a girl, I always loved candles and sparkling lights. Part of the magic of the Christmas time is its brilliance as a season of lights. Since childhood, I have sometimes visited different denominational worship services. I especially liked ones that had special candle lighting services. I must admit that I just had an instinctive feeling about how the candles seemed to connect with worship, but I gradually have learned more and more about the reasons. There are many candle traditions connected with Christmas. Some people put candles in windows to indicate a family member is away or as a welcoming to friends or travelers. I have seen several explanations for the use of the seven candles associated with Christmas. Of course, the number seven is considered to mean wholeness and perfection. It follows that seven would be a good number of candles to select. I especially like the tradition that says the seven candles symbolize (1) Christ as the light of the world, (2) the honoring of His love for the world, (3) remembering the gift of children and family, (4) honoring armed forces personnel who protect our freedom to worship, (5) remembering the preciousness of friends, (6) remembering and guiding us to help those who are in need, and (7) remembering and guiding us to help those who suffer and feel alone in the world. The lighting of seven candles could truly be a meaningful Christmas prayer. The last candle of these mentioned does remind me of my Christmas card. I sense that its inspiration comes from a realization and remembrance of the reality that the beauty of a snowy scene, in fact, still cannot totally erase the coldness, darkness, and loneliness of a lost world. Yet, our Lord Jesus Christ came so that His love, warmth, and light can shine brightly breaking all the negativity by His saving grace. We do need so much to let His Light shine through us at Christmas and every day. Perhaps, candle traditions help us to remember what is needed.

For example, the Advent candles and wreath symbolize the spirit and gift of Christ's birth and gift to the world. I do like services where families take part in the lighting of these candles, helping us to remember the meaning of the season. *Advent* is from the Latin, *adventus*; *arrival* or *coming* are the translations that perhaps best fit this season. Traditions for lighting and the number of candles have changed over time and may vary among cultures and families. Supposedly, such traditions date back to the fourth and fifth centuries. One tradition has the use of a wagon wheel decorated to display the candles. I didn't learn the meanings of the items that make up the wreath part of these displays until fairly recently. I can see how the circular wreath made from sharp greenery represents the crown of thorns worn by Christ. These wreaths often have red decorations that were, probably once and maybe still are, the red berries of the holly used for the greenery, illustrating the blood Christ shed. I used to wonder about the significance of pine cones at Christmas (the cones are the coverings that release seeds to the wind), but now I can see that these symbolize the seed of the new life we can receive by Christ's sacrifice, death, and resurrection. I have noticed that as I began more and more to connect Christmas not only with His coming but also with His purpose in coming that I find myself learning more how the traditions that make this connection originated. Unfortunately, I am concerned that today we embrace such traditions without understanding their original meanings. I learned that sometimes people have and do still use candles for each day of December leading up to Christmas. I suppose the Advent calendar takes the place for many people, eliminating the need to light all those candles. I have a wooden case that opens into a nativity scene that serves as my Advent calendar. Characters are added each day to complete it. A picture of it is included in the collage that I posted earlier in the book. Perhaps, I should add some candles around it this coming year. I am most familiar with the use of the purple candles with a single pink candle. A white candle is often added on Christmas Eve. I haven't read this point but wonder about the progression from purple to white and if it symbolizes how our fleshy nature becomes infused by His love so that we can move more to the purity that He brought through His sacrifice for us, drawing us to His pure light. I do treasure the reminder that His Advent brings the promise of His gifts of hope, peace, joy, love, and life now and forever as the Advent candles symbolize.

Many candles add much warmth, comfort, and light. Nevertheless, I do like to focus on the significance and meaning of each single light. I have many candles around the house. Most of these are no longer the burning type but the battery powered ones. I just don't trust myself with too many real candles. I have one set on a coffee table that has special significance because my grandchildren, when they were small, liked to take the small candles out of their separate container and turn them on, carefully replacing each candle to shine through the glass. One grandson in particular loved to set to this task upon his arrival. Now, I even have a few candles that I can turn on with a remote control. The problem with these electronic candles is that they require frequent battery replacements. The specialness for me of the single candle traces back to a church I often visited in the evening with a neighbor friend. The whole service was about prayer and lighting a candle for a personal, special prayer. How I treasure those memories and those of worship in other countries where I have prayed and lighted candles. I have been privileged to be in churches and cathedrals in other countries. Most were built with love and understanding of how important Christ and His Light are. Sainte-Chapelle at the right time of day for sunlight illuminates in a way that is indescribable, filling one with awe and a spirit of worship. Chartres radiates not only with the subtle light through the stained glass but also with its depiction of the Bible in glass and stone. Notre Dame was a masterful work of love that instilled a sense of worship, prayer, and understanding. I feel so privileged to have seen it one last time just before the fire. I was able to share this experience with some grandchildren, lighting candles for prayer. I was amazed how these young children spotted details of spiritual significance as they examined pictures and carvings. This was a joyous time. In contrast to that joy, during a time of personal conflict, I was blessed to be in Saint Peter's Basilica in Rome. It was a dark and rainy day that matched my spirit of despair. I was under the skylight inside when suddenly the sun broke through, shining brightly on me. I felt an answer to prayer and a revived spirit. How I treasure that moment. There are many others places of worship that I could mention, but these are particular cathedrals that I had so wanted to visit for a Christmas Eve service. However, after years of spiritual growth and after an event I will share shortly, I treasure any place to celebrate our Lord's coming. It is very special to be in a small church as people turn out the lights, light single candles, and sing "Silent Night" softly, reminding us that "all is bright." "Then Jesus spoke to them again, saying, 'I am the light of the world. He who follows Me shall not walk in darkness, but have the light of life'" (John 8:12, NKJV). No matter where I am only one thing really matters: the Lord Jesus Christ came and lives today to bring His Light into the darkness. Because of this fact, we must let Him light our candle and let it shine. Yes, I can have light even if I am alone on a dark, snowy night similar to the picture on my card.

I have noticed that cards are not sent as they once were. I understand that the cost of a card and the mailing becomes a problem. I do try to save cards. I must admit that I pull out ones from the past because I like to see cards even though fewer and fewer new ones arrive each year. The cards may have decreased but the stockings have increased. The one thing that I love about having a staircase is that I can line it with all the stockings that I need as more grandchildren and great grandchildren arrive. Many times my children or grandchildren will bring a friend. I believe that I mentioned previously that I like to have a stocking for anyone who is with me for Christmas celebration. I like to put fun gifts in these. Coming up with new, interesting ideas for stockings is more challenging with each passing year. I say Christmas celebration because I have given up the idea of having these times actually on Christmas Eve or Christmas Day. With married children and grown grandchildren, finding a time for a gathering is seemingly impossible. I am happy if sometime during the season I can have as many of them together at one time as possible. I was hoping that I would not have to experience a virtual gathering this year. However, I did and found it was wonderful seeing them even if not in person. My plan for the stockings in that event seemed to work. Things have changed for the Christmas season, but one thing has never changed: the gift of God in the sending of His son. Love truly came down. "For God so loved the world that He gave His only begotten Son, that whoever believes in Him should not perish but have everlasting life. For God did not send His Son into the world to condemn the world, but that the world through Him might be saved" (John 3:16-17, NKJV).

Not having people around on Christmas Eve, Christmas Day, and the decorating for Christmas has been one of my personal spiritual challenges. I probably would love to have a Christmas House. As I am writing, I can see my nutcrackers ranging from small to large still at the base of the stairs.

Yes, these, along with one nativity scene that I mentioned earlier, and two Christmas trees are still visible. One tree is small and up high over a closet door. Another is standing with a few decorative ornaments remaining on it; however, the silver balls have been packed away. It is not the decorations so much as the warm memories that are attached to these decorations. These memories include the few sad times, the many fun, festive times, and the deeply spiritual times. This brings me to the true reason that I am writing.

For some time, I felt lead to write about one very special Christmas. The nudging has ranged from soft to pressing. I have avoided doing this writing as long as possible because it is extremely personal spiritually. Although many might believe me to be outgoing, I am actually shy by nature. I often avoid some encounters and, especially, confrontations. This sharing will most certainly produce skepticism and, perhaps, even raised eyebrows and confrontations. However, I must now share no matter the consequences. "He *is* a shield to all who trust in Him" (Psalm 18:30, NKJV).

This particular Christmas looked to be an exceptionally exciting one for that period. Of course, I would later discover with the arrival of many more grandchildren and great grandchildren that the more the merrier and that each new grandchild added joy upon joy. How I do digress, perhaps I am attempting to avoid this account. The house was decorated, special food was prepared, and family members were scheduled for Christmas Eve and Day. A forecast for snow meant that we might even have a white Christmas. Such expectations can be a foreshadowing of ultimate disappointment. Snow did arrive, only early. It began snowing heavier and heavier. Soon flights were cancelled and roads were closed. The feast, presents, and decorations so carefully prepared would not have guests to enjoy them. The snow was beautiful but the house was empty. Only my husband and I sat there alone on Christmas Eve with no likelihood that the weather would improve for days. I saw my husband's face wanting to do something to make things better yet knowing that there was nothing he could do for me. I felt deep sadness, but then from the depths of this sadness, I sensed the Spirit moving within me, moving me towards truth and understanding. I was to experience a most undeserved outpouring of love—the true meaning of the season.

I withdrew to my bed, partly because it would be warmer and partly because I knew that I needed quiet time with the Lord. As I shared my sadness and disappointment with Him, I felt His love and comfort but also instruction. The message of this season was about Him. He came, giving up all the glories of Heaven to have a lowly existence, to be mistreated, to be misunderstood, to be tortured, and to be crucified. All of this, He did so that the world and myself could be offered the joy of His salvation and presence now and forever through eternity. His birthday that we celebrate was about what He gave, just the opposite of what we would consider a birthday. I had been focusing on joy and peace from what I received from all the excitement, gift giving, and celebrations. Of course, what I enjoyed most was the giving to and doing for others, but my focus was not where it should be. I quietly wept as I thought about how misplaced my thinking, focus, and heart had become. My heart filled with regret and repentance. I was keenly aware of all the errors of my past, present, and probably even future. I was reminded that His sacrifice covered them all and that He would remember them no more. He came to save and not to condemn. I felt His love, His arms wrapped around me. I didn't deserve this love, but He gave it at a time when I should have been praising and glorifying Him, but instead, I had selfishly been feeling sorry for myself. (Romans 8:32-39, NKJV): "He who did not spare His own Son, but gave Him up for us all—how will He not also, along with Him, graciously give us all things? Who will bring any charge against those whom God has chosen? It is God who justifies. Who then is the one who condemns? No one. Christ Jesus Who died—more than that, Who was raised to life—is at the right hand of God and is also interceding for us. Who shall separate us from the love of Christ? And No, in all these things we are more than conquerors through Him who loved us. For I am convinced that neither death nor life, neither angels nor demons, neither the present nor the future, nor any powers, neither height nor depth, nor anything else in all creation, will be able to separate us from the love of God that is in Christ Jesus our Lord."

Then, something miraculous occurred. Suddenly, I was swept up. I believe it was in the spirit only. It was as though my body remained. I do not believe that this was a dream but that it was a reality. The reader can determine what they believe or do not believe. That discussion is for you and the Lord. I was carried above the Earth and through the stars and galaxies. I saw wonders upon wonders that I cannot begin to describe. I cannot begin to explain the closeness, the warmth, the peace, and the joy that I experienced. Soon, I was back in my bed, still sitting up and filled with warmth, peace, and joy. I experienced a special closeness to my Lord and Savior. He, again, gave on His birthday. He gave me a Christmas that I will never forget—a Christmas that I could never deserve. A very personal Christmas filled with His presence and His love—to me, a most undeserving sinner. He gave me His Christmas birthday visit.

Later, as I thought back upon this experience, I remembered two episodes from life that connected beautifully with this Christmas miracle experience. One would send me back again to my childhood. This one would spur memories of warm summer days and nights. You see most of my childhood was without air conditioning. Dad would rig his makeshift swamp cooler later on, using the cold well water to help with the summer heat. However, prior to that time, summers found me outside in the cooler and whimsical world of my treehouse. I would spend days up there reading books checked out from the library. I loved the trip with mother, usually on the bus, to downtown and the marvelous library. That library with its large staircase, floors with books and resources no longer exists. I would later spend many nights and weekends there doing research for school papers. I would use the card catalogue, the stacks of magazines and newspapers, and later the magic of microfiche. As a child, I had learned to use the card catalogue and the helpful personnel to find books to check out for my days in my treehouse.

I was not alone when in my special treehouse place. I taught my dog to climb a ladder so he could join me. Unfortunately, these lessons meant that we would hear from neighbors that our dog was on their roof. When he saw a ladder, he climbed it. My cat naturally found its way into my treehouse. Along with books would be food, animal treats, and water. One summer my entire reading consisted of books about astronomy and outer space. At night, I would look at the night sky, marveling at its wonderland. With virtually no city lights, the night sky produced its own unique light show. I would sometimes talk to the Lord during these times, many times sharing what I was wondering about as I read and observed. "The heavens declare the glory of God; And the firmament shows His handiwork" (Psalms 19:1, NKJV).

The other episode also involved a wondrous sky event. Let me first provide more background for this episode. I had once so wanted to go into space. I must admit that I have long been thrilled by space shows. In fact, I recently was given a few "May the 4th be with you" birthday parties, making the play on the words and my birthday. Before my Christmas visit, I had even thought about entering the contest to select a teacher to go into space. In 1984, a program connected with NASA offered classroom teachers an opportunity to go into space. I seriously considered entering the contest because of my deep desire to see all the wonders of space and all the majesty of Earth from space. Guided by the Spirit, I knew that I should not. I had children who needed me and students who depended upon me.

The decision to teach was not necessarily one that I had originally embraced. I wanted to be a missionary, but the Lord lead me "kicking and screaming" in a different direction. I digress; all of these discussions are for another time. I did become a teacher and fell in love with teaching and my calling. Although I did not enter the contest, I continued to follow all of the information and details about it. While in Colorado, I had a waking vision that startled me and would haunt me for some time. I saw a rocket ship launching into the sky only to explode into flames. I looked at those around me for reactions. I saw no reactions. I asked them if they saw anything in the sky. They responded no with questioning looks. Thinking that perhaps the altitude had played tricks on me, I returned home and to work.

I remember telling a few of my students about the strange incident, wondering if any of them had experienced issues at high altitudes. I also remember being troubled. I wondered if I should try to contact NASA because the launch would soon take place. Of course, they would think I was crazy because I was beginning to think that I was. This thinking turned to a sickening feeling and deep regret when students who were watching the Challenger launch in science class came after class to my room to tell me what had happened. For years, I carried a gnawing sense that I did not try to say or do anything. I did know that I was glad that I did not enter the contest. My conscience was soothed later as I learned that others did warn NASA about the launch. Even the warnings of engineers did not stop the launch. What remained for me was to pray for families of those lost and anyone who felt a sense of guilt about that tragic day.

What did these events mean? What was I to think, or most importantly, to learn? I know that my Christmas experience gave me a wonderful peace and sense of presence of my Lord and Savior. I know that I did not merit any of this peace or glimpses beyond what I ever could have seen even in a spaceship into the heavens. I know that I begin a deeper understanding of God's majesty, plans, timing, and mysteries. I know that I realize I do not need to spend time in worrying, fretting, and trying to plan, "not leaning on my own understanding."

I know that I learned that Christmas is about my Lord's gift to the world. We cannot out give Him. Although I still enjoy the trappings of Christmas and, especially, those times with ones whom I love, the day belongs to the Lord. I can sit by myself in a Christmas Eve service where everyone around me has family, knowing that I am not alone. I have extra joy at children's services, especially if those include grandchildren, praying that all receive His love and joy as a child. My Lord is with me, has been with me, and will be with me forever. I know that truly "…He shall give you the desires of your heart." (Psalm 37:4b, NKJV)

My wish this and every season is that everyone could accept the Lord Jesus as their personal Lord and Savior. My prayer is that everyone could know that love, joy, and peace He brings, working gently, either swiftly or over the years, to help one to learn, know, understand, and trust. I pray that everyone accept His free gift of Himself. We truly need to remember that His birth was and is a Christmas birthday visit from Heaven for yesterday, today, and evermore.

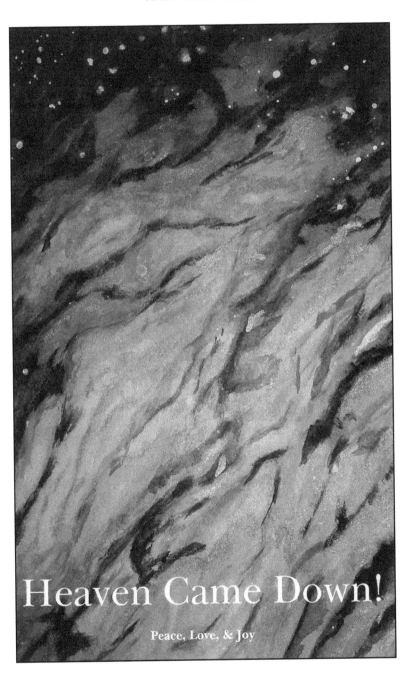

Heaven Came Down!

Peace, Love, & Joy

Heaven came down
That Christmas night
Bringing joy, peace, and
Everlasting light!

May each of you
This Christmas time
Receive God's gift of
Salvation sublime!

This is the bread which comes down from heaven. If anyone eats of this bread, he will live forever; and the bread that I shall give is my flesh, which I shall give for the life of the world. John 6:50-51 NKJV

CPSIA information can be obtained
at www.ICGtesting.com
Printed in the USA
LVHW020744021121
702212LV00011B/313

9 781637 695340